THE AWESOME POWER OF VOLCANO

FOR
OF NA

BY CATHERINE O'N

, EARTHQUAKES, AND TORNADOES

CES
TURE

L GRACE   NATIONAL GEOGRAPHIC   Washington, D.C.

FOR MY UNCLE ROBERT DECKER, VOLCANOLOGIST EXTRAORDINAIRE —COG

Published by the
National Geographic Society

John M. Fahey, Jr.,
*President and Chief
Executive Officer*

Gilbert M. Grosvenor,
Chairman of the Board

Nina D. Hoffman,
*Executive Vice President,
President of Books and
Education Publishing Group*

Ericka Markman,
*Senior Vice President,
President, Children's Books
and Education Publishing
Group*

Staff for this book:

Nancy Laties Feresten,
*Vice President,
Editor-in-Chief,
Children's Books*

Bea Jackson,
Art Director, Children's Books

Marfé Ferguson Delano,
Project Editor

David M. Seager,
Designer

Janet Dustin,
Illustrations Editor

Carl Mehler,
Director of Maps

Mark A. Wentling,
Indexer

R. Gary Colbert,
Production Director

Lewis R. Bassford,
Production Manager

Vincent P. Ryan,
Manufacturing Manager

Copyright © 2004
National Geographic Society

Published by the
National Geographic Society.
All rights reserved.

Reproduction of the whole
or any part of the contents
without written permission
from the National Geographic
Society is strictly prohibited.

Printed in Belgium

Library of Congress Cataloging-in-Publication Data

Grace, Catherine O'Neill, 1950-
Forces of nature : the awesome power of volcanoes, earthquakes, and
tornadoes / by Catherine O'Neill Grace.
    v. cm.
Includes index.
Contents: On the rim of a live volcano—In the zone of an earthquake—
In the path of a tornado.
ISBN: 0-7922-6328-6
   1. Volcanoes—Juvenile literature. 2. Earthquakes—Juvenile
literature. 3. Tornadoes—Juvenile literature. [1. Volcanoes. 2.
Earthquakes. 3. Tornadoes.] I. Title.
   QE521.3.G7 2004
   551.2—dc22

                               2003018929

Printed in Belgium

The typeface used in this
book is Bookman.
Display type was illustrated
by Bob May, based on title
treatment for the film
Forces of Nature.

This book is a companion
to *Forces of Nature*, a giant-
screen film from National
Geographic and Graphic Films.

The film *Forces of Nature* is
presented by Amica Insurance
and funded in part by the
National Science Foundation.

Graphic Films

Credits
All photographs in this book are from the giant-screen film *Forces of
Nature* except as noted below: Front cover, Tsuyoshi Nishinoue/Orion
Press; Introduction, w. faidly.weatherstock.com; 12, Vincent J. Musi;
14 (top), National Geographic Maps; 14-15, Pierre Mion; 16, Richard
Alexander Cooke III; 24 (left), Swim Ink/CORBIS; 24 (right), CORBIS;
25 (upper), Vincent J. Musi; 26, U.S. Geological Survey; 32-33, Wayne
McLoughlin; 35 (upper), Rykoff Collection/CORBIS; 35 (lower),
Bettmann/CORBIS; 36, Tom Bean/CORBIS; 39, Reuters NewMedia
Inc./CORBIS; 40-41, Reuters NewMedia Inc./CORBIS; 46-47, Greg
Eliason; 51, Precison Graphics; 58 (top), National Geographic Maps; 58
(bottom, left to right), courtesy of Joshua Wurman, Richard Herd,
Marie Edmonds, Ross Stein

Front cover: Created by friction from swirling ash, lightning crackles
over Japan's Sakurajima volcano.
Back cover: A tornado touches down near Aberdeen, South Dakota.

Quotes
All quotes from the scientists featured in this book are from
interviews conducted by the author, which are cited in the Resources
section on page 60.

Acknowledgments
The author and the publisher thank Dr. Marie Edmonds, Dr. Richard
Herd, Dr. Ross Stein, and Dr. Joshua Wurman for so generously
sharing their time and expertise. We also are grateful to Erica Immucci
of National Geographic Television and Film for her invaluable
assistance with this book.

This material is based in part upon work supported by the National Science
Foundation under Grant No. ESI-0205992. Any opinions, findings, and conclu-
sions or recommendations expressed in this material are those of the author and
do not necessarily reflect the views of the National Science Foundation.

CONTENTS

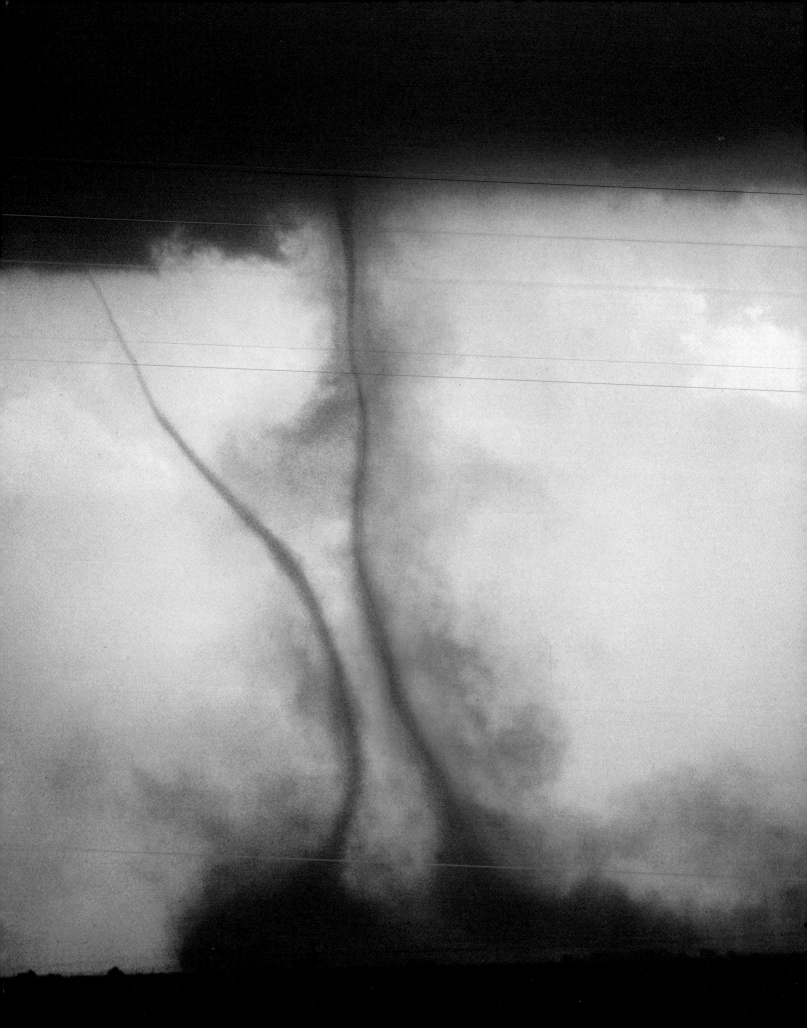

The ground beneath our feet usually feels solid and reliable. But huge forces of nature can change our familiar planet and cause great destruction. Earthquakes shake the surface, bringing buildings crashing to the ground. Volcanoes erupt, sending melted rock down hillsides and burning ash into the air. Currents in the atmosphere can spin into devastating tornadoes that blow down houses and businesses, and turn cars and trucks into piles of twisted metal.

The Department of Homeland Security's Federal Emergency Management Agency (FEMA) knows very well the destruction that these natural disasters can bring. We are working on ways to build communities that will help reduce the risk of damage to people and property. But there is still much that we don't know about how natural disasters occur and when they will strike. Scientists are working hard on these questions, hoping that the answers will help save lives, houses, other buildings—indeed whole communities. These scientists have a dangerous job. They may work right on the edge of a live volcano or in an active earthquake zone. They may even put themselves right near the spinning, deadly funnel of a tornado!

The scientists whose work is featured in this book and in the large-format film *Forces of Nature* share a passion to understand Earth and to use what they are learning to help people. We at FEMA applaud their efforts to help predict and prepare for the disasters that occur in this nation and around the world every year.

Michael D. Brown

Michael D. Brown
Under Secretary of Homeland Security for Emergency Preparedness and Response

ON THE RIM OF A LIVE

VOLCA

NO

In October 1997, the eruption of Soufriere Hills volcano on the Caribbean island of Montserrat filled the air with billowing clouds of debris. Scientists had predicted the eruption, so the people living on the island were able to get out of the way of the dangerous explosion.

A ghost town when this photograph was taken in 1996, Plymouth, the once bustling capital city of Montserrat, lies just below the smoking Soufriere Hills volcano. The city's residents fled when the volcano began erupting in 1995.

The helicopter sweeps closer and closer to the smoking crater. The dedicated scientists riding in it peer through the ash and steam to observe the dome of lava bulging inside the crater. When will the volcano erupt? That's what volcanologists Marie Edmonds and Richard Herd are hoping to predict. Mission accomplished for the day, the helicopter banks away from the heat and ash and flies back to the relative safety of the Montserrat Volcano Observatory on the volcano's flank.

Why would anyone choose to live right on the slopes of a live volcano? Because a volcano that is constantly changing and erupting makes an amazing laboratory for studying earth science. The Montserrat Volcano Observatory (MVO) is located on Montserrat, an island in the eastern Caribbean, an area of the world with about 25 active volcanoes. The observatory, sited about four miles northwest of the volcano, is run by the government of Montserrat.

Montserrat's Soufriere Hills volcano is one of the world's most active. After centuries of quiet, the volcanic peak started steaming, shaking, and growing in 1995, and it has been active ever since. In 1997, a huge eruption devastated Plymouth, the island's capital. Superheated surges of gas, ash, and lava blocks raced down the volcano's slopes, destroying everything in their path. Luckily, the 11,000 people who lived in Plymouth were given advance warning by scientists at the MVO. They had safely evacuated the town, moving to the north side of the island. But their homes, stores, and schools were incinerated by the eruption.

Dr. Edmonds, Dr. Herd, and their colleagues are in a risky profession. But they consider themselves lucky to live and work on a part of Earth's surface where volcanic activity can be seen up close.

Wearing protective gear, Marie Edmonds (below, left) and Richard Herd, volcanologists from the Montserrat Volcano Observatory, take measurements of the chemicals in gases and ash spewed from the volcano's crater.

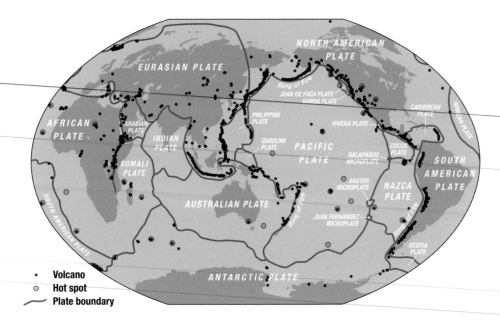

- • Volcano
- ◎ Hot spot
- ⌒ Plate boundary

Earth's crust is divided into gigantic slabs called tectonic plates, indicated by purple lines in the diagram at left. The red dots indicate volcanoes, and the yellow spots signal hot spots—places where magma burns through a plate. Under the island of Montserrat, the North and South American plates slip under the Caribbean plate, creating what geologists call a subduction zone (below). In this zone, the rock that forms the plates melts and becomes magma. This super-heated molten rock rises in columns to the surface and forms a dome. Eventually, heat and pressure build to the bursting point, and an eruption happens (right).

How do volcanoes form? The energy that fuels them comes from deep within the Earth. Earth is made up of three layers. The outer layer, which is called the crust, is made of solid rock. It ranges in thickness. In places beneath the ocean, for example, it is only about 6 miles deep; in other places it is some 40 miles deep. This rocky crust is broken into large sections that geologists call tectonic plates. Earth's middle layer, known as the mantle, is very hot—hot enough to melt rock! The core is the innermost layer of Earth. It is even hotter than the mantle.

Hot, melted rock within the mantle is called magma. Near plate boundaries and where Earth's crust is thin under the ocean floor, magma rises to the surface, seeking a place to break through. The melted rock can gush or ooze through cracks or holes in the crust, creating volcanoes. Once the magma has broken through the surface, geologists call it lava.

Carribean Plate

North American Plate

Montserra

Crust

Mantle

Magma

Magma chamb

South American Plate

Subduction

Steam and gases

Active dome

Old domes

Ash flow

Old ash flows

Movement of plate
bduction zone

This cutaway view of
Montserrat's Soufriere Hills
volcano shows the active
dome, as well as three domes
that were formed during
previous periods of activity.

The heat and energy in the mantle create forces that slowly nudge the giant rocky plates of the crust around the globe, as though they were on a large conveyor belt. At their edges, the plates collide, grind past each other, or pull apart. Enormous stress builds up along plate boundaries, and sometimes this energy is released in the form of earthquakes or volcanoes. Most of the volcanoes on the Earth's surface are found at places where plates meet. As plates bump into each other, the edge of one can bend and slip beneath the other one. When that happens, some of the rock bends down into the mantle, where intense heat melts it. This melted, or molten, rock rises back toward the surface, where it may break through to form a volcano.

Magma also bubbles up out of the mantle along lengthy faults—cracks in the crust—where plates pull apart. There molten rock hardens and forms long undersea mountain ranges. In some places, these volcanic mountains rise high enough from the ocean floor to break through the surface of the ocean and create islands, such as those in Hawaii. As the scientists who live on Montserrat know so well, volcanoes can be extremely dangerous. As magma rises to the surface, it can break blocks of rock, causing earthquakes. Hot, sometimes poisonous, gases can erupt to the surface, too. Rocks and debris can explode with tremendous force from vents, or openings in the volcano. Fires start, trees are felled, and buildings in the path of volcanic material are burned by or engulfed in lava, or buried in mounds of volcanic ash.

By understanding how volcanoes develop, scientists hope to be able to predict their behavior more accurately. The most important mission of the scientists at MVO is to

DID YOU KNOW...

■ that more than 80% of the Earth's surface is volcanic—including areas of the seafloor?

■ that there are about 500 active volcanoes on Earth's surface—not counting the volcanoes under the sea?

■ that the largest volcanic eruption in modern times happened in 1912 at Novarupta, Alaska? For 60 hours in June of that year, 3.6 cubic miles (15 cubic kilometers) of magma exploded from the Earth— about 30 times the material that erupted from Mount St. Helens in 1980.

On the Big Island of Hawaii, red-hot lava bubbles and fountains from the crater of Kilauea volcano. Kilauea has been spouting lava since 1983. Often occurring at the edges of tectonic plates, volcanoes are found all over the globe.

watch the volcano and warn people on the island if another major eruption is about to happen. To do this, they conduct complex scientific observations. Dr. Edmonds, who earned her Ph.D. at Cambridge University in England, studies the gases that escape from the volcano. Dr. Herd, who earned his Ph.D. at Lancaster University in England, measures ground deformation, the changes in the volcano's shape and size. Deformation of the volcano's surface happens as the volcano responds to changes in pressure deep inside the magma chamber, the pool of superheated molten rock that powers its eruptions. The top and sides of the volcano can actually swell up or sink down as conditions in the chamber change.

"We measure earthquakes and gas emissions and observe how the ground is deforming," Dr. Edmonds explains. "We monitor these things constantly to try to forecast what the volcano will do next. Then we evaluate the risks posed by various volcanic hazards on this island."

Earthquakes caused by the restless volcano are recorded in the field by devices called seismometers. These are located in 14 places around the volcano. Powered by a combination of batteries and solar energy cells, the seismometers transmit data to computers at the observatory 24 hours a day. Often, drifting volcanic ash covers the surface of the solar cells and the scientists have to go out and wipe them off. "We need to keep the remote sites clear so that they will keep working in a crisis," says Dr. Edmonds.

Montserrat's volcano is fascinating to watch, as well as to study, says Dr. Edmonds. "We get to study this volcano on our doorsteps. It's such a small island, and the volcano is ever present. Everyone is aware of it all the time. We can sit at our computer terminals collecting data, look out the window, and watch pyroclastic flows."

Superheated volcanic material called a pyroclastic flow races down Soufriere Hills volcano.

■ that a kind of volcanic rock called pumice can be so light and porous that it will float in water? Pumice is created when frothy magma solidifies on contact with air.

■ that between 1980 and 1990 volcanic activity around the world forced nearly 450,000 people to flee their homes?

■ that the explosive booms from the huge 1883 eruption of Krakatau, a volcano in Indonesia, were heard in Australia, 2,200 miles away?

Pyroclastic flows—sometimes called *nuées ardentes*, which is French for "glowing clouds"—are incandescent mixtures of volcanic fragments and gases that are emitted from a volcano and sweep along the ground. Depending on conditions, such as the angle of a volcano's slope, the flows can zoom downhill very fast and be extremely destructive and deadly to anything in their path.

"When I was at school I was always interested in geology and volcanoes," Dr. Edmonds says, "even though there are no active volcanoes back in England. I studied physics and math and physical geology, and did my graduate work looking at the geochemistry of gases."

At MVO, Dr. Edmonds has plenty to study. "The volcano is erupting most of the time," she says. In addition to the data crunching the scientists do at their computers, they use a helicopter to observe the volcanic dome located within the crater at the top of the volcano.

"We use the helicopter for flying quite close to the volcano," says Dr. Edmonds. "We can see which parts of the dome are active. We also use it to get to and maintain our field sites."

Dr. Edmonds has lived and worked on Montserrat for two years now. She says the volcano offers a window into the interior workings of our planet. "Volcanoes are one way our planet loses heat," she says. "They allow us to see the way the rock that forms its surface is recycled. They can also be very beautiful. At night we can see the flows glowing in the dark."

Her position at MVO, and her life on Montserrat, is very different from working in a lab at a university and living in a city. "There are not very many shops and restaurants," Dr. Edmonds says, noting that Montserrat's small capital city, Plymouth, was destroyed in the 1997 eruption. "But it's an amazing opportunity to be here."

In 2004 Dr. Edmonds and Dr. Herd's research will take them to another part of the world, to the Hawaiian Volcano Observatory in Hawaii Volcanoes National Park, to work for the United States Geological Survey.

In addition to observing ground deformation on Montserrat, Dr. Herd surveys the volcano's lava dome. Dr. Herd says that he chose to study volcanology because "it's the most dynamic part of geology. It's an exciting science with much to teach us about the Earth."

Scientists at Montserrat Volcano Observatory keep a daily log of the volcano's behavior. Just how dynamic and exciting the volcano can be is recorded in this observation from the summer of 2001:

"July 01: Major collapse of the eastern flank of the dome occurred. The event began at 5:00 pm and lasted for a period of 8–9 hours, producing near-continuous pyroclastic flows down the Tar River valley to the sea.

In a helicopter, Richard Herd heads back to the lab after taking a close look at the crater atop Soufriere Hills volcano. He checked the lava dome within the crater. Swelling could signal pressure building toward an eruption.

These four photographs of the Soufriere Hills volcano show an explosion in progress in October 1997. During this time, volcanic material burst from the volcano frequently, sending ash clouds 40,000 feet into the air and spewing fragments of volcanic rock all over the island.

Mt. St. Helens

On a sunny morning in May 1980, a lovely, snowcapped peak in Washington State exploded. Until that spring, Mount St. Helens had been dormant, or inactive, for 123 years. But the volcano began to awaken. In March, geologists began to notice signs that something big was going to happen. Dozens of earthquakes began to shake Mount St. Helens. A 300-foot bulge formed on the side of the mountain. The peak of the volcano began to steam and smoke. Then, on May 18 at 8:32 a.m., the huge eruption began. The blast tore away a portion of the peak equal in height to the Empire State Building. By the time it was over, the eruption had killed 60 people and devastated 150 square miles of forest, leaving behind an ashy wilderness. Today, nearly 25 years later, life has begun to return to the slopes of the volcano. Wildflowers bloom, and wildlife has returned. But Mount St. Helens is not asleep. Although the volcano has not erupted since 1985, geologists at nearby Johnston Ridge Observatory observe frequent releases of steam and other signs that prove hot magma still lies within.

Extensive areas around Long Ground were affected by pyroclastic surges. Strong southeasterly winds carried ash as far away as Puerto Rico and the Virgin Islands. Approximately 45 million cubic meters (59 million cubic yards) of the dome were removed and the summit region lowered by about 250 meters (820 feet)."

Dr. Herd says that although the volcano makes a remarkable lab for scientists, the eruptions, which began in 1995 and show no signs of stopping, have been "tragic for the island." Many citizens of Montserrat have been driven from their homeland, their homes burned and their fields buried by volcanic material. They have had to relocate to other islands. Today, fewer than 4,000 people—including the staff at MVO—remain on the island. Some 8,000 have left.

About half of Montserrat's citizens evacuated to the northern hills, out of the path of ash and gas flows. Some had their homes trucked to safer areas.

Based on the actual event, this scene from the film *Forces of Nature* re-creates the thick clouds of ash that filled the streets of Montserrat in 1997 as citizens escaped to places out of the path of the dangerous debris spewed by the Soufriere Hills volcano.

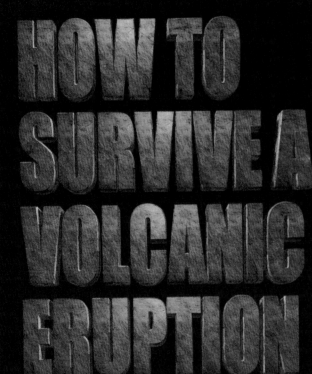

HOW TO SURVIVE A VOLCANIC ERUPTION

WHAT SHOULD YOU DO IF YOU ARE IN AN AREA WHERE A VOLCANO BEGINS TO SPEW LAVA, ASH, AND GAS? THE SCIENTISTS AT MONTSERRAT VOLCANO OBSERVATORY IN THE WEST INDIES HAVE THE FOLLOWING ADVICE:

DURING AN ERUPTION

- Stay away from the volcano. DO NOT try to go have a look!

- If you are outdoors, avoid areas downwind of the volcano. Winds can carry poisonous gases and ash for miles.

- Seek shelter indoors.

- Avoid low-lying areas where poisonous gases can collect.

- Beware of mudflows. These can happen when hot ash and lava melt snow atop volcanoes. The liquid mixes with soil and forms fast-moving rivers of mud.

AFTER AN ERUPTION

- Protect your skin by wearing pants and long-sleeved shirts.

- Use goggles to protect your eyes from gritty ash and a dust mask or damp cloth to cover your face and help you breathe properly. Inhaling volcanic ash is dangerous. It contains harmful chemicals.

- Listen to a radio for emergency instructions.

"We're into year nine of surveying and measurement here, and there's no sign of a letup," Dr. Herd says. "It looks as if it might go on for a long time. Our job here is to track and monitor the activity and make a record."

Located on the northwest side of the volcano, the MVO is in a relatively safe place "unless there was a monstrous event," Dr. Herd says. Even so, he admits, the volcano's power can be frightening at times. "You look up and see this thing looming up above you. And when you're up in the helicopter it's incredible. When we fly close, the heat can boil the paint on the outside of the helicopter."

In spite of the isolation and possible hazards, Dr. Herd says, he's grateful for the chance to work at MVO. "There's no glitz and casinos on Montserrat, but it's incredibly interesting. Not many folks have their office windows looking out at a volcano."

Although clouds of ash often hang in the air, everyday life continues on Montserrat. Here a team plays cricket within sight of the Soufriere Hills volcano.

Modern apartment buildings in the nearby city of Adapazari lie crushed and uninhabitable following the powerful earthquake that shook Izmit, Turkey, in August 1999. The quake killed thousands of people as they slept.

IN THE ZONE OF AN

EARTH

QUAKE

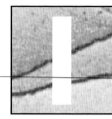stanbul is in danger. Cracks in the Earth's crust lie near this Turkish city and stretch beneath the Sea of Marmara nearby. These cracks, called faults, could trigger a devastating earthquake, threatening the 13 million people who live in the crowded, ancient city. Here, American geologist Ross Stein and his Turkish colleagues are racing against time, trying to decipher clues in Earth's crust. They know quakes will occur in this endangered region someday—likely someday soon. They would like to be able to learn to predict where and when so that people's lives can be saved.

Scientists know that earthquakes happen when the huge plates of rocky crust that form our planet's surface move suddenly. Along their boundaries, plates are split by many cracks, called faults. The edges of the plates are rough and can get stuck as the plates grind past each other. The forces within the Earth's mantle that move huge plates of crust around the planet's surface bend, or deform, the rocks along fault lines. As rock bends, energy builds within it, much as energy is stored in a

The domed Hagia Sofia (right) has survived earthquakes in Istanbul since the sixth century. Scientists study the building for clues about making safer structures. Several million people live in the earthquake-prone city today, crowding its streets and buildings, including the Grand Bazaar (far right).

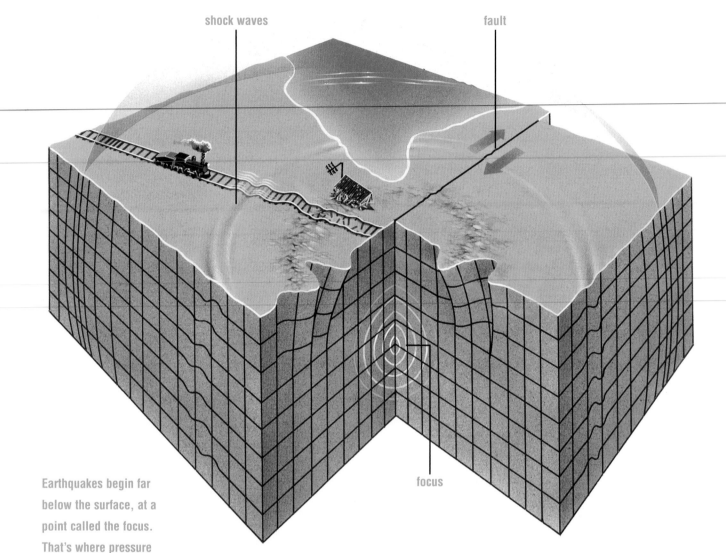

shock waves   fault

focus

Earthquakes begin far below the surface, at a point called the focus. That's where pressure along a fault causes it to snap. Shock waves spread out from the focus and move through the rock. As they go, the waves push and pull on the crust. They heave the surface up and down and from side to side. This motion can tumble buildings and bend railroad tracks.

rubber band when you stretch it. When the plate can no longer resist the energy, the edges unstick along the fault and the rocks snap and slip forward, similar to the way a stretched rubber band snaps back to its original shape when you let it go. The fault unzips at a speed of about 5,000 miles per hour, shedding waves of energy, called shock waves, that move through the Earth's crust, shaking the ground as they go. Earthquake!

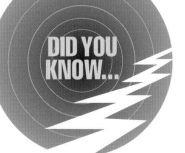

Earthquakes are the most deadly of all natural disasters. It's hard to imagine the huge shock waves they release moving through solid rock in the way ripples move through water. But that's just what the waves do. Their energy shakes the Earth and everything on it. Depending on their strength, shock waves, also called seismic waves, cause the solid material of the crust to crack, crumble, jerk, shake, collapse, and split apart. Earthquakes can turn buildings into rubble, snap bridges in two like toys, and open gaping cracks in the surface of major highways. In the resulting chaos, many people may be injured, left homeless, or even killed.

Geologists use seismometers and other instruments to measure the movements of the Earth during an earthquake. With today's equipment, including precise Global Positioning Systems (GPS) that measure surface movement from satellites, scientists can study the occurrence of earthquakes along a particular fault. They may even be able to forecast where the shaking

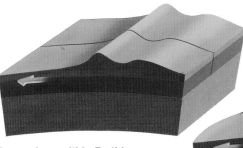

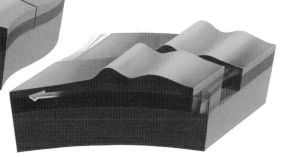

Forces deep within Earth's hot mantle exert pressure on the rocky plates of the crust, causing them to move. These diagrams show what happens as two plates struggle to slide past each other along a fault. Energy begins to build.

The edges of the slabs may catch and lock as they move along the fault. Stress builds. The rock on each side of the fault slowly deforms, or bends, storing up more energy.

Finally, rock on one side of the fault jerks past the other side, sending out shock waves. Earthquake!

will occur. But they can't predict when it will happen or how strong it will be. For example, in 2003 the U.S. Geological Survey forecast that a powerful and damaging earthquake of magnitude 6.7 or greater has a 62 percent chance of striking the San Francisco Bay area during the next 30 years. That's a potentially devastating event for a region with a population of some seven million, including 764,000 in the city of San Francisco. So far, this is the closest scientists can come to saying when the quake will happen. Lack of a more precise timetable makes saving people and property from the destructive power of earthquakes difficult. And since earthquakes cannot be accurately predicted, says Dr. Stein, we must instead learn to live with them, by making buildings stronger and preparing emergency plans.

There are several ways to measure an earthquake's power. The moment-magnitude scale, which evolved from the Richter scale created in 1935 by a California geologist, is the one used most today. Earthquakes that measure below 4 on the moment-magnitude scale usually do not cause damage. Those below 3 usually can't be felt by people, although they can be measured by seismometers.

Earthquakes from 4.9 to 5.4 on the scale can be felt, but cause only slight damage. Magnitude 5.5 to 6 earthquakes can rock trees and cause some structural damage to buildings. Magnitude 6.1 to 6.5 earthquakes can cause poorly constructed buildings to collapse. Earthquakes that measure above 6.5 can cause serious damage in widespread areas. Earthquakes from 8 to 9 on the scale are termed "great." They can knock down buildings within a hundred miles of where the quake occurs. An earthquake that measures more than 9 on the scale is very rare. It can cause damage for hundreds of miles around. (A magnitude 9 earthquake is a thousand times

THE GREAT SAN FRANCISCO EARTHQUAKE

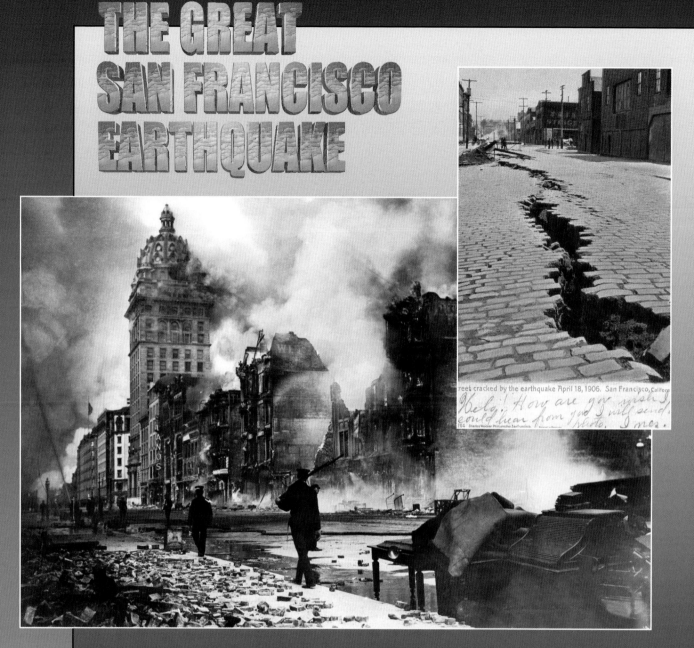

reet cracked by the earthquake April 18, 1906. San Francisco, Califor

Help! How are you wish I could hear from you I will send photo. I mea.

204 Charles Weidner Photographer San Francisco

San Francisco was a young and vibrant city in 1906. Some 400,000 people were living there when, at dawn on April 18, the ground began to shake. The earthquake lasted for 45 seconds, rippling streets like ribbons and collapsing buildings. Soon fires began as stoves and kerosene lanterns fell over. The flames spread quickly, engulfing the city's many wooden houses. By the time the shaking stopped and the fire was out, 28,000 buildings had been destroyed, an estimated 3,000 people had died, and more than half the population of the city was homeless. Scientists estimate that the quake measured 7.7 on the moment-magnitude scale. That day the Earth trembled as far north as Oregon, as far south as Los Angeles, and as far east as Nevada. Still called the Great San Francisco Earthquake, the event remains one of the worst natural disasters ever to hit the United States.

stronger than a magnitude 7 and a million times stronger than a magnitude 5 quake.)

Experiencing an earthquake is something people never forget. For Ross Stein, feeling the power of a quake helped him decide to become a geologist. He grew up in Los Angeles, where he experienced the 1971 San Fernando earthquake. "Going through a situation where solid ground turns to Jell-O is amazing," Dr. Stein says. "You never forget it!"

"I went to Plantation Camp, a summer camp, from the age of 8 to 16," Dr. Stein says. "It straddled the San Andreas Fault, about a hundred miles north of San Francisco. That camp is sacred ground to me. There were lots of fault features—even a tree that had been split in two and offset three feet in the 1906 earthquake. But both sides are still living! While I was in college at Brown University, I spent my spring break back west at Plantation studying the effects of the 1906 earthquake, and I saw the place with new eyes. Every time I come back I see more of its history etched into the landscape."

In college, Dr. Stein says, he discovered that being a geologist allows you to get outside and travel to fascinating areas as you try to find out things about the Earth. "When I was an undergraduate I studied planetary geology," he recalls. "But I wanted to work on an area where I felt I was doing something for people. I still wanted to make discoveries about the Earth, but I wanted them to be ones that could contribute to people's lives." After earning his Ph.D. at Stanford University in Palo Alto, California, Dr. Stein decided that the study of earthquakes and a job with the U.S. Geological Survey was the answer. At the USGS, he works as a geophysicist—a geologist who studies the Earth's strain, deformation, and earthquake history. "This work is driven by an attempt to deepen our understanding of earthquakes and to develop a new way to make hazard assessments," he says. "We are hunting for clues to how one earthquake sets up the next."

Most Americans have heard about the San Andreas Fault in California. Less familiar is the North Anatolian Fault, which comes within ten miles of Istanbul and stretches across northern Turkey. But Dr. Stein knows the Anatolian Fault well. He has been traveling to Turkey for many years to work with Turkish scientists who are studying the complex system of cracks in the crust.

The North Anatolian Fault is extremely active. There were ten magnitude 6.7 earthquakes along it between 1939 and 1992. The detailed history of these events makes the area a laboratory for studying how large earthquakes transfer stress along faults, creating the conditions for a future quake. (These lessons from the Anatolian Fault also help Dr. Stein understand the San Andreas Fault, which is nearly its twin in structure.)

In 1997 Dr. Stein and his Turkish colleague, the late Aykut Barka, published the results of their study of the ten earlier quakes that had occurred along the North Anatolian Fault. They showed that each quake had increased stress in an area next to it along the fault. And they took a chance by doing something that geologists rarely do. They forecast that the next quake would likely strike either the eastern city of Erzincan or the western city of Izmit.

They were right.

In August 1999, a magnitude 7.4 earthquake struck Izmit. The quake caught most people as they slept. The 37 seconds of shaking pancaked, or collapsed, 14,000 poorly constructed apartment buildings and blocked major highways. Both cellular and landline phone systems were knocked out. A major fire broke out in an oil

Residents of Izmit survey the damage following the 1999 earthquake. The powerful quake collapsed buildings, blocked roads, and interrupted communications, making it difficult for rescuers to reach the devastated city.

refinery when a huge chimney rocketed into the ground. The blaze it sparked burned for five and a half days, filling the sky with dense black smoke. The earthquake killed thousands of people. Rescuers from around the world poured into Izmit to try to help, although most of them arrived too late to do more than console and shelter the survivors.

Among the survivors Dr. Stein interviewed was a woman who had lost 150 members of her extended family in the quake. He also talked to a couple who had been trapped in their bed in the ground floor of a flattened building for three days, until they were rescued by a mountain climber. Their young son died. Dr. Stein has many other such stories.

Survivors of the Izmit earthquake wear masks to avoid inhaling the dust and debris from structures reduced to rubble by the quake.

When a quake strikes, small things can make the difference between life and death. "We found that if you survive the collapse of a building you can shout for several hours, but eventually your voice gives out," says Dr. Stein. "If you have a whistle, you can whistle forever!" Dr. Stein lives near the San Andreas Fault in California. "We have put whistles on our kids' backpacks," he says, "and my wife and I have whistles on our key chains. It's a way to help ensure that you can be rescued. No one is going to drill through concrete unless they are sure that someone is alive on the other side."

The magnitude 7.4 quake in Izmit was a terrible human disaster. The much smaller magnitude 6.6 earthquake that struck the southeastern Iranian city of Bam in December 2003 was similarly devastating. It killed at least 30,000 people and left an estimated 40,000 homeless.

Scientists like Dr. Stein and his colleagues are worried that a great many more lives could be lost if a quake strikes along the North Anatolian Fault near the city of Istanbul, with its population of 13 million people. He believes that it is the part of our planet with the largest concentration of people at imminent risk for an earthquake.

"Istanbul has a history of earthquakes," Dr. Stein explains. "In its 2,000-year history there have been 12 large ones. There is a fascinating written record going back all those centuries. Through that time one building—the huge, domed Hagia Sofia—has remained standing for 1,500 years." Originally built as a church, then converted into a mosque and now functioning as a museum, Hagia Sofia has survived and been restored after every quake. "It's like a

Viewed here from inside the building, the circular shape of Hagia Sofia's dome, which distributes stress to its outer edges during an earthquake, helps explain why the structure has survived earthquakes for centuries.

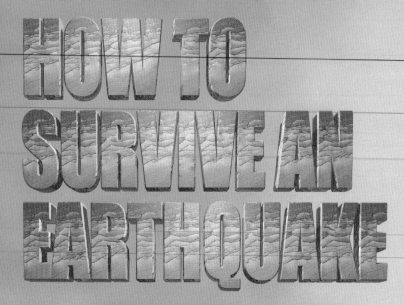

HOW TO SURVIVE AN EARTHQUAKE

KIDS WHO LIVE IN EARTHQUAKE ZONES LEARN WHAT TO DO WHEN THE EARTH TREMBLES. THEY EVEN HAVE EARTHQUAKE DRILLS AT SCHOOL. THEY ARE TAUGHT TO "DROP, COVER, AND HOLD ON!" WHEN THE SHAKING BEGINS. TO STAY SAFE DURING AN EARTHQUAKE, FOLLOW THIS ADVICE FROM THE AMERICAN RED CROSS:

- If you are indoors, seek shelter in a safe place such as under a sturdy table or desk or against an inside wall where nothing can fall on you.

- If you are in bed, hold on and stay there, protecting your head with a pillow.

- If you are outdoors, find a clear spot away from buildings, trees, and power lines. Drop to the ground.

- When you have found shelter, hold on tight, and protect your eyes by pressing your face against your arms.

The American Red Cross also advises families who live in earthquake zones to pack survival kits and keep them in a visible place at home. They should include:

- A first aid kit with essential medication, including prescriptions

- Canned food and a nonelectric can opener

- At least 3 gallons of water for each member of the family

- Protective clothing, rainwear, and bedding or sleeping bags

- A battery-powered radio, flashlight, and extra batteries

- A whistle

giant seismometer," Dr. Stein says. "We can figure out the intensity of those ancient earthquakes from the record of what has happened to Hagia Sofia."

The other reason Hagia Sofia interests Dr. Stein so much is that he sees it as proof that Istanbul's buildings can be redesigned to withstand future earthquakes. Its domed roof and flying buttresses—special structures that provide support—spread stress around in such a way that the building resists falling down, the way so many flat-roofed buildings do.

"Hagia Sofia never fell down," Dr. Stein says. "If a 1,500-year-old building can survive multiple earthquakes, then surely a modern apartment building reinforced with steel should be able to survive a quake undamaged. A future earthquake need not be a death sentence. The question is, can people build at least as good a building as Hagia Sofia?

"Istanbul has made some efforts to prepare [for a big earthquake]. There is an early-warning system so sirens might blare tens of seconds before a major earthquake. There has been a modest retrofit of existing buildings, and there is increased awareness about what you need to do to survive. But all this has to be measured against the 850,000 buildings in the city, of which perhaps three-quarters are collapse risks."

Dr. Stein and other scientists feel a great sense of urgency about figuring out how to prepare Istanbul for an earthquake. Geologists fear that a big quake in Istanbul would kill many more than the 25,000 to 40,000 people who died in Izmit. Scientists like Dr. Stein are trying to persuade people in Turkey—and in other parts of the world where earthquakes threaten—to build cities that will stand up to the colossal forces of nature.

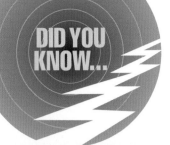

DID YOU KNOW...

that most states in the U.S. experience earthquakes? Only four states—Florida, Iowa, North Dakota, and Wisconsin—had no detectable earthquakes between 1975 and 1995.

that Alaska is the most earthquake-prone state in the U.S.? Our northernmost state is shaken by a magnitude 7 quake almost every year.

that the world's deadliest earthquake happened in 1557 in central China? The quake struck where people lived in caves carved from soft rock. These collapsed, killing some 830,000 people.

IN THE PATH OF A
TORNA

Two large tornadoes roar across flat fields near Aberdeen, South Dakota, in June 2002. The plains of the central United States are prone to powerful storms that have earned the region the nickname "Tornado Alley."

They sound like freight trains roaring straight toward you. They surge and race across the landscape, swirling with wind, picking up dust and debris as they go. They are capable of leveling everything in their path. They are tornadoes, Earth's most powerful storms, and they pack an incredible punch. Ask Joshua Wurman. He was there in Bridge Creek, Oklahoma, on May 3, 1999, when mobile radar trucks recorded tornado wind at speeds of 301 miles per hour. That's the fastest wind ever recorded near Earth's surface!

When tornadoes race across the landscape, most people rush for cover. And that's a good idea, because tornadoes are extremely dangerous. Not meteorologist Josh Wurman, however. When some of the world's most dangerous weather hits, he heads right toward it.

"I call it running the wrong way," Dr. Wurman says. "It's not as dangerous as it looks. We know what we're dealing with and how the tornadoes behave. We're the world's experts on this, and we have the world's best tools. Every few seconds the radar gives us an update on what's happening."

Tornadoes develop from energy released in thunderstorms. They are most common in the central plains of North America, where they appear most often in spring and summer. But tornadoes have occurred in every one of the United States, on any day of the year. They also sometimes happen in other parts of the world, on every other continent except Antarctica.

Scientists know more about these destructive storms

When Josh Wurman decided to mount weather-radar equipment on a truck, Doppler on Wheels (DOW)—and the science of studying tornadoes up close and personal—was born. Here, two of his colleagues stand outside a DOW and scan the skies.

DID YOU KNOW...

■ that the single most destructive tornado ever recorded in the world was the Tri-State Tornado in 1925? On March 18 that year, the tornado developed in Missouri, headed next into Illinois, and then traveled to Indiana. It destroyed four towns and killed 695 people as it raced along a 219-mile-long track.

■ that tornadoes kill an average of 60 people a year in the United States? Most of the deaths are caused by flying debris or collapsing buildings.

■ that tornadoes can last from several seconds to more than an hour?

than ever before, but they still don't know exactly how they form. That's what sends Dr. Wurman out into the field every year to try to catch and record tornadoes.

"Weather is a young science," says Dr. Wurman. "And storm research is a new science. Weather in general has a lot of very big questions that still need to be answered and that are kind of in our faces every day. One of the biggest questions is, what causes a tornado? We don't really know. What causes lightning? We don't have good answers yet. So it's a very challenging and rewarding science."

Meteorologists do know that tornadoes form in powerful thunderstorms called "supercells." As these storms start to rotate, they spawn more intense, smaller rotating currents called tornadoes. But so far, scientists can't predict exactly when and where the tornadoes will form, or how big they will be, or how long they will last.

Luckily, 90 percent of tornadoes are relatively weak. But the other 10 percent are terrifying, destructive forces of nature that cause billions of dollars in damage.

A gigantic thunderstorm, like this one on the East Texas plains in spring 2001, can pack swirling wind currents that spawn tornadoes. When these massive storms, called supercells, begin to revolve, meteorologists get ready to issue tornado warnings.

A tornado begins when circular winds develop deep inside a storm cloud. Moving downward, the winds form a twirling tunnel. Winds near the ground pick up dust and debris, forming a dark cloud around the tornado.

WELCOME TO TORNADO ALLEY

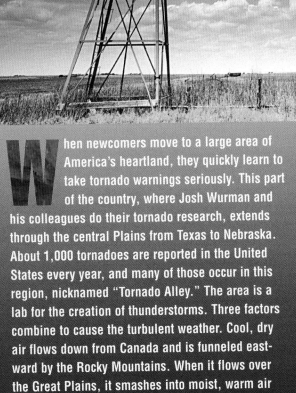

When newcomers move to a large area of America's heartland, they quickly learn to take tornado warnings seriously. This part of the country, where Josh Wurman and his colleagues do their tornado research, extends through the central Plains from Texas to Nebraska. About 1,000 tornadoes are reported in the United States every year, and many of those occur in this region, nicknamed "Tornado Alley." The area is a lab for the creation of thunderstorms. Three factors combine to cause the turbulent weather. Cool, dry air flows down from Canada and is funneled eastward by the Rocky Mountains. When it flows over the Great Plains, it smashes into moist, warm air that has boiled up from the Gulf of Mexico. A layer of dry air between the cold currents aloft and the moist air at the surface acts like the lid on a pressure cooker, locking in energy. The energy builds up, eventually exploding into powerful thunderstorms that can breed tornadoes.

Dr. Wurman, who earned his Ph.D. at the Massachusetts Institute of Technology (MIT), did not grow up in tornado country. He's from Philadelphia. He says he was very interested in weather throughout his childhood. He even built his own backyard weather station to measure rainfall and temperature.

"I like weather," he says. "When I was a kid in first grade I used to cut out newspaper pages about the weather and summarize them for the school newsletter. I have always been very interested in math and physics. I was a nerd, and this was a way to apply my interests as an adult."

As an adult, Dr. Wurman has pursued—literally—his interest in tornadoes. He lives in Boulder, Colorado, where he heads the Center for Severe Weather Research.

Scientists used to think that measuring the winds inside a whirling tornado was impossible. The powerful storms destroyed the equipment before any signals could be recorded. But Dr. Wurman didn't give up. He developed a new radar device that can measure many sections of a tornado's funnel cloud and translate that information into a three-dimensional computer image—a portrait of a tornado. Called the Doppler on Wheels, or DOW, Dr. Wurman's invention consists of radar dishes and other special equipment mounted on trucks.

Driving the DOWs, Dr. Wurman and his colleagues race around the countryside in tornado weather, trying to get close enough to the storms to measure and map what's going on inside them. At a distance of less than two miles from a tornado, the equipment from one DOW sends out radio waves to scan the winds inside the twister. A second DOW scans the tornado from another angle. Together, the DOWs provide enough data to make three-dimensional models of the winds and assess their speed.

DID YOU KNOW...

■ that the vertical winds in tornadoes can lift objects as heavy as railroad cars right off the ground?

■ that tornadoes have picked up and deposited objects in all kinds of odd places? In 1950, near Clyde, Texas, a small refrigerator was carried half a mile and lodged at the top of a telephone pole!

■ that tornadoes can carry lightweight objects such as papers high up into the atmosphere, where upper level winds can carry them for hundreds of miles?

When a powerful tornado blew through Aberdeen, South Dakota, on June 24, 2003, this house didn't stand a chance. The winds swirled the structure into splinters, leaving a bathtub near the top of the heap.

HOW TO SURVIVE A TORNADO

WHEN A TORNADO IS COMING, YOU NEED TO ACT FAST TO BE SAFE. THANKS TO EARLY-WARNING SYSTEMS, TODAY PEOPLE IN TORNADO COUNTRY ALMOST ALWAYS HAVE ENOUGH TIME TO SEEK SHELTER. TAKE TORNADO WARNINGS SERIOUSLY! IF A TORNADO STRIKES, THE MOST IMPORTANT THING YOU CAN DO IS PROTECT YOURSELF FROM FLYING DEBRIS, REPORTS THE FEDERAL EMERGENCY MANAGEMENT AGENCY (FEMA). HERE'S HOW:

- Stay away from windows!

- If you have time, get to a storm shelter located in a school, church, or other public building.

- At home, retreat to the basement and get under something sturdy, such as a work bench or a staircase.

- If there is no basement, go to an inside room without windows on the first floor—a bathroom or a closet. The idea is to put as many walls between yourself and flying debris as you can.

- If there is no time to get indoors, lie down flat in a ditch or low area. Use your arms to protect your head and neck.

- If you're in a car or truck, do not try to outdrive a tornado. Stop, get out of the car, and immediately take shelter in a nearby building. If there is no time to get indoors, get out of the car and lie in a ditch or low-lying area away from the vehicle.

Make sure your family has a storm-survival kit. It should contain things you will need if your house is damaged or if your electricity is off for a long time:

- a safe light source such as light sticks and a battery-powered lantern or flashlight. Avoid candles, which could start a fire.

- a battery-powered radio

- extra batteries

- a high-quality pocket tool that includes pliers, a screwdriver, a cutting blade, and a wirecutter

- a fire extinguisher

- a first aid kit

Dr. Wurman and his colleagues create exact images. But finding a tornado to measure and model is far from an exact science. It's a hit-or-miss business, says Dr. Wurman. He and his team forecast the general area where tornadoes are likely to form. Then they drive there and wait to see what happens, hoping to place their radar near enough to gather data. Often, the tornadoes will pop up far from the scientists and their equipment. They rev their engines and speed off again, on the trail of another storm. No wonder the team logs 10,000 miles on the DOWs every spring.

"We have about a 25 percent success rate. Seventy-five percent of the time the tornadoes don't form—or sometimes they form miles away." When they do find a storm, there's not much time to be scared. "It's pretty busy and tense out there," he says. "We don't have time to yell, 'Wow!' The minute a tornado forms I wish I could say 'Wow!' but I'm too busy doing my job. I am trying to get all the equipment positioned correctly to take measurements, and I'm looking at my computer screen."

Dr. Wurman says, "It's important to learn better ways to forecast when and where a tornado is going to form. My work is directly rewarding. There are real benefits to people. I am working on problems that can be solved, and it won't take a hundred years to do it. The first tornado we caught and got radar data on—that was one of the best days of my life. I have a rare opportunity to be able to make a significant contribution."

After tornado season, Dr. Wurman spends time refining his equipment and studying his data. But when spring weather breeds new storms, he and his colleagues are back in the DOWs again, chasing funnel clouds in their quest to figure out some of the unanswered questions about the force of nature we call tornadoes.

DID YOU KNOW...

■ that the central United States experienced a record-breaking week of tornadoes from May 4 to May 20, 2003? During that time, some 384 tornadoes occurred in 19 states, causing 42 deaths.

■ that the largest radar-documented tornado happened in Mulhall, Oklahoma, on May 4, 1999? At one point, the tornado was more than a mile wide.

■ that deaths caused by tornadoes have been steadily dropping in recent decades? This is due to better warnings and public awareness of dangerous storms.

ON LOCATION

SCIENTISTS MARIE EDMONDS, RICHARD HERD, ROSS STEIN, AND JOSHUA WURMAN PREFER TO WORK AS CLOSE AS POSSIBLE TO THE DESTRUCTIVE FORCES OF NATURE THEY STUDY. THIS MAP SHOWS WHERE THEY CONDUCTED THE RESEARCH FEATURED IN THIS BOOK.

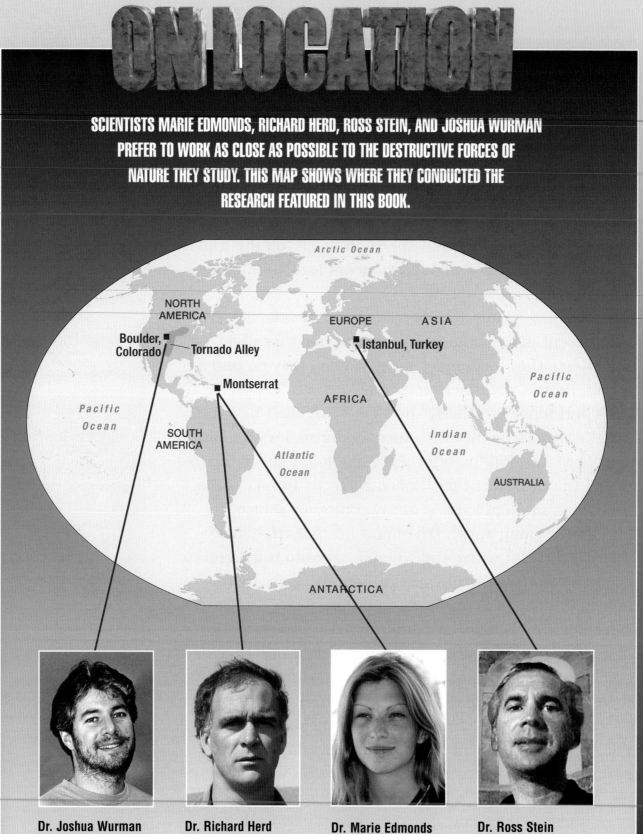

Dr. Joshua Wurman
Meteorologist
Boulder, Colorado

Dr. Richard Herd
Volcanologist
Montserrat

Dr. Marie Edmonds
Volcanologist
Montserrat

Dr. Ross Stein
Geologist
Istanbul, Turkey

active volcano: a volcano that is currently erupting

aftershocks: small tremors that follow the largest shock of an earthquake over a period of weeks, months, or even years

ash: a fine powder of tiny jagged particles of volcanic rock

core: the innermost layer of the Earth

crater: a depression in the summit of a volcano from which lava flows originate

crust: the rocky, outermost layer of the Earth

dome: a rounded bulge of sticky lava that forms in the crater when magma rises from within a volcano

Doppler radar: a radar system that uses radio waves to measure wind speed and direction in storms. Named for a 19th-century Austrian scientist who studied the behavior of waves, it is a vital weather-forecasting tool.

dormant volcano: a volcano that is quiet, not currently erupting, but that may erupt sometime in the future

earthquake: an abrupt shift of rock along a fault, or crack, in Earth's crust that causes the ground to shake

epicenter: the point in the Earth's crust directly above where an earthquake begins

eruption: the expulsion of gases, ash, volcanic fragments, or lava from a volcano onto the Earth's surface

extinct volcano: a volcano that was active at some time in the past, but is not expected to erupt again

funnel cloud: a rotating cloud that is not in contact with the ground. When a funnel cloud touches down on the ground, it is classified as a tornado.

geologist: a scientist who studies the Earth and its structure

Global Positioning System (GPS): a system that uses signals from satellites to precisely locate positions on the Earth's surface

ground deformation: changes in the shape and size of a volcano that indicate that magma is rising inside

lava: molten rock erupted onto the Earth's surface from a volcano

magma: hot, melted rock below the surface of the Earth that may rise to the Earth's surface and be erupted at a volcano

magma chamber: a space beneath the Earth's surface that contains magma

mantle: the layer of the Earth that is between the crust and the core

meteorologist: a scientist who studies the weather

nuées ardentes: a French term for pyroclastic flow. It translates as "glowing clouds."

pyroclastic flow: a mass of gases, hot ash, and larger blocks of lava that flows rapidly down the sides of a volcano

seismic wave: movement that passes through and shakes the Earth's crust when stress is released in an earthquake

seismometer: an instrument used to measure the shaking of the Earth's crust during an earthquake

supercell: an extremely intense thunderstorm with strong rotating winds that can breed tornadoes

tectonic plates: rigid sections of crust that drift very slowly across the surface of the Earth

tornado: a twisting funnel of low-pressure air that emerges from some severe thunderstorms, gathering speed and touching down on the Earth's surface with winds up to 300 miles an hour or more

vent: an opening in the Earth's crust through which ash, gases, or lava might erupt

volcano: a vent in the Earth through which lava, gases, and ash reach the surface. A volcano often takes the form of a mountain or hill around a vent.

volcanologist: a scientist who studies volcanoes

Bibliography

Allen, Missy, and Michel Peissel. *Dangerous Natural Phenomena.* New York: Chelsea House, 1993.

Bluestein, Howard B. *Tornado Alley: Monster Storms of the Great Plains.* New York: Oxford University Press, 1999.

Bolt, Bruce A. *Earthquakes.* New York: W.H. Freeman and Company, 1999.

Bolt, Bruce A. *Inside the Earth.* New York: W.H. Freeman and Company, 1982.

Brumbugh, David S. *Earthquakes: Science and Society.* Upper Saddle River, New Jersey: Prentice Hall, 1999.

Bunce, Vincent. *Volcanoes.* Austin, Texas: Steck-Vaughn Company, 2002.

Decker, Robert, and Barbara Decker. *Volcanoes.* New York: W.H. Freeman and Company, 1998.

Galiano, Dean. *Tornadoes.* New York: The Rosen Publishing Group, 2000.

Harrison, David L. *Volcanoes: Nature's Incredible Fireworks.* Honesdale, Pennsylvania: Boyds Mills Press, 2002.

McCann, Janice, and Betsy Shand. *Surviving Natural Disasters.* Portland, Oregon: House Calls Books, 1995.

Mogil, Michael H. *Tornadoes.* Stillwater, Minnesota: Voyageur Press, 2001.

Sutherland, Lin. *Earthquakes and Volcanoes.* Pleasantville, New York: Reader's Digest Books For Children, 2000.

Wade, Nicholas, editor. *The Science Times Book of Natural Disasters.* New York: The Lyons Press, 2000.

Winchester, Simon. *Krakatoa: The Day the World Exploded: August 27, 1883.* New York: HarperCollins, 2003.

Interviews

Edmonds, Marie. Interviewed by the author. Telephone and e-mail exchanges, April 2003.

Herd, Richard. Interviewed by the author. Telephone and e-mail exchanges, April 2003.

Stein, Ross. Interviewed by the author. Telephone and e-mail exchanges, April 2003.

Wurman, Josh. Interviewed by the author. Telephone and e-mail exchanges, April 2003.

Internet Sources

American Red Cross
www.redcross.org
This organization steps in to help whenever and wherever disaster strikes. Check their Web site for information on how to be prepared in advance.

Center for Severe Weather Research
www.cswr.org
This site publishes Josh Wurman's latest observations of tornadoes from the Doppler on Wheels (DOW) project.

Federal Emergency Management Agency
www.fema.gov/kids
This U.S. government agency responds when natural disasters such as earthquakes, hurricanes, and tornadoes strike. Check out FEMA for Kids for information about how to be prepared for disasters.

Montserrat Volcano Observatory
www.mvo.ms
This Web site provides daily updates, including video footage, of activity on Soufriere Hills volcano. Check out the education section for information geared to kids.

National Oceanographic and Atmospheric Administration (NOAA)
www.noaa.gov
This site covers weather around the United States. Look for special sections on tornadoes and volcanoes, and be sure to visit NOAA for Kids at www.education.noaa.gov.

National Severe Storm Laboratory
www.norman.noaa.gov
This lab leads the way in the investigation of severe storms and hazardous weather to improve forecasts and save lives.

United States Geological Survey (USGS)
www.usgs.gov
This government organization gathers information about the geology of the United States. Check out their special sections about earthquakes and volcanoes for amazing facts, maps, videos, and more. Go to http://earthquake.usgs.gov/4kids to see activities and information geared to kids.

USGS Earthquake and Volcano Deformation and Stress Triggering Research Group
http://quake.usgs.gov/~ross
Click on the Teaching Materials icon on this Web site to see a variety of demonstrations from Ross Stein's classroom, including an "earthquake machine." Other sections in the site include interactive maps and charts of earthquake fault zones.

INDEX

Illustrations are indicated in **boldface.**

A
Adapazari, Turkey 28, **28–29**
Alaska
  earthquakes 33, 45
  volcanic eruptions 17

B
Bam, Iran
  earthquake 42
Bridge Creek, Oklahoma
  tornadoes 49
British Geological
  Survey 13
Buildings
  earthquake-resistant
    30, **30,** 42,
    43, 45

C
California
  earthquakes 34, 35,
    37, 42
  see also San Andreas
    Fault, California
Center for Severe
  Weather Research,
  Boulder, Colorado
  53
Chile
  earthquakes 33
China
  earthquakes 45
Crust see Earthquakes;
  Faults; Subduction
  zones; Tectonic
  plates

D
Doppler on Wheels
  (DOW) **48–49,** 49,
  53, 57
Dunkley, Peter **18**

E
Earthquakes 28–45
  buildings resistant to
    30, **30,** 34, 42,
    43, 45

caused by volcanoes
  18
causes of 17, 30,
  32–33
damages from 33, 34,
  35, 38–41, 42
deaths caused by 28,
  41, 45
diagrams **32, 33**
facts about 33, 42, 45
focus 32
measurement of 33,
  34, 37
prediction of 30,
  33–34, 38
shock waves 32–33,
  42
survival tips 42, 44
warning systems 45
  see also Shock waves
Edmonds, Marie 13, **13,**
  18, **18,** 20, **58**
Eruptions, volcanic **16,**
  26
  advance warnings 13,
    18
  diagram **15**
  predictions of 9,
    17–18
  survival tips 26
  see also Pyroclastic
    flows

F
Faults 17, 30, 32–33
  diagrams **32, 33**
  see also North
    Anatolian Fault;
    San Andreas
    Fault, California

G
Global Positioning
  System (GPS) 33
Grand Bazaar, Istanbul,
  Turkey **31**
Great San Francisco
  Earthquake (1906)
  35, 37

H
Hagia Sofia (building),

Istanbul, Turkey 30,
  30, 42, **43,** 45
Hawaii
  volcanoes **16,** 17, 27
Hawaiian Volcano
  Observatory 21
Helicopters
  used to survey volca-
    noes 13, 20, 21,
    21, 27
Herd, Richard 13, **13,**
  21, **21,** 27, **58**

I
Iran
  earthquake 42
Istanbul, Turkey **31,** 38
  earthquakes 30, 42,
    45
  see also Hagia Sofia
Izmit, Turkey
  building damages 38,
    39–41
  earthquake (1999) 28,
    38, 40–41, 42
  oil refinery 38, **39,** 41

K
Kilauea (volcano), Hawaii
  16, 17
Krakatau (volcano),
  Indonesia 20

L
Lava 14, **16, 26**

M
Magma 14, **14–15,** 17,
  18, 20
Mantle 14, 17, 30, 33
Martinique
  volcanoes 27
Mauna Loa (volcano),
  Hawaii 27
Moment-magnitude
  scale 34, 37
Montserrat (island), West
  Indies see Soufriere
  Hills Volcano,
  Monserrat
Montserrat Volcano

Observatory (MOV)
  13, 17–18, 20, 27
Mount St. Helens,
  Washington 17, 24,
  24

N
North Anatolian Fault,
  Turkey 38, 42

O
Ocean floor
  volcanoes 14, 17, 27
Oklahoma
  tornadoes 49

P
Plymouth, Montserrat
  12, **12,** 13, 20
Pumice 20
Pyroclastic flows 18, **18,**
  20, 21, 25, 27

R
Radar see Doppler on
  Wheels (DOW)
Richter Scale 34

S
San Andreas Fault,
  California 33, **36,**
  37, 38, 42
San Francisco,
  California
  earthquakes 34, 35,
    35, 37
Seismic waves see
  Shock waves
Seismometers 18, 33, 34
Shock waves 32–33, 42
Soufriere Hills Volcano,
  Monserrat **12, 21,**
  27
  eruption (1997)
    10–11, 11, 13,
    20, **22–23,** 23
  helicopter observa-
    tions of 13, 20,
    21, **21,** 27
  pyroclastic flows 18,
    18, 21, 25

One of the world's largest nonprofit scientific and educational organizations, the National Geographic Society was founded in 1888 "for the increase and diffusion of geographic knowledge." Fulfilling this mission, the Society educates and inspires millions every day through its magazines, books, television programs, videos, maps and atlases, research grants, the National Geographic Bee, teacher workshops, and innovative classroom materials. The Society is supported through membership dues, charitable gifts, and income from the sale of its educational products. This support is vital to National Geographic's mission to increase global understanding and promote conservation of our planet through exploration, research, and education.

For more information, please call 1-800-NGS LINE (647-5463) or write to the following address:
National Geographic Society
1145 17th Street N.W.
Washington, D.C. 20036-4688 U.S.A.
Visit the Society's Web site at www.nationalgeographic.com.